VISIONS, BREATHS AND SIGHS

Paola Cannas

Augur Press

ISBN 978-0-9932182-0-0

First published 2015 by
Augur Press
Delf House
52 Penicuik Road
Roslin
Midlothian EH25 9LH
United Kingdom

Printed by Lightning Source

VISIONS, BREATHS AND SIGHS

Acknowledgements

Translator: Bernard Wade, Dublin, Ireland and Lucca, Tuscany

These poems were originally published by Felice Editore, Pisa, in *Respiri e sospiri*, 2013

Contents

Introduction

Introduction

In the summer of 2012, Paola Cannas, by then in her 80s, invited her son, Marco Vichi, to dine with her. At that meeting, she asked him if he would read two of the poems that she had written. She wanted to know if they were any good, and whether or not he liked them. As he read them he was moved to tears by their beauty, simplicity, honesty and goodness, and he felt sad that he had not known his mother in this way before. He subsequently collected together all her poems, some written on scraps of paper, others in old jotters, all of them scattered in drawers and boxes around her home.

Marco , a well-established author, wanted to be certain that his mother's poems were valued in their own right – 'walking on their own legs' as he said. He identified a possible publisher in Pisa – *Felici Editore* – but did not at first reveal that the poems had been written by his mother. He received a very quick response to say that the poems would be published. *Respiri e Sospiri* – 'The little big book', as it became known in Italy – was received with tumultuous applause across the country. When Marco told his mother that the poems were to be published, she said, 'I only wanted to see if *you* liked them. Do you mean they liked them too?' Shortly before she died, Paola was interviewed by the Florence newspaper *Corriere Fiorentina*.

These beautiful poems were written at various stages throughout Paola's life. Using freeform verse, she draws the reader into each situation and experience with some of the clarity, depth of vision and gentle affection with which she was gifted. These poems speak for themselves.

Paola Cannas was born in Lucca in 1928, and lived all her married life in Florence (Tuscany). She died in her beloved Tuscany on 17 March 2013. She had very deep feeling for Sardinia – the land of her forebears.

*　*　*　*　*

I translated these poems almost immediately after reading them. I had been so moved by them that I wanted my wife and friends to be able to read them, too. Paola's dying wish was that any possible proceeds from publication of her poems should go to charity. Her son, Marco, nominated *Il Filo di Juta* (The Jute Thread), which, based in Florence, builds schools in Bangladesh. In 2014, a school to teach literacy to the children of Bangladesh was renamed 'The Paola Cannas School'. Having read the translated poems, Augur Press wanted to make them available to the English-speaking world.

Bernard Wade, translator,
Dublin, Ireland and Lucca, Tuscany, April 2015.

*　*　*　*　*

When we received the first sample of the translated versions of Paola Cannas' poems, we knew immediately that this material carried a depth of focus that is rare. And we knew that the poems had been translated by someone who loved and really *felt and experienced* them in both their original language and its translation. Meaning can be lost in the process of translation, but in this case, the poetry has retained the original vital message – sometimes gentle, sometimes forceful, always powerful, filled with truth and spiritual wisdom.

Mirabelle Maslin, Augur Press, April 2015.

POEMS

Life is nothing without friendship

Cicero

La vita non è nulla senza l'amicizia

Cicerone

FRIENDS

By now the living
are no longer beside you
and do not keep you company;
in vain you try to keep
their gaze upon you,
to squeeze their hand in yours.

Their eyes turn elsewhere,
their fingers close on their palms,
urgency makes distant their steps.

But look here on the edge of your bed,
they sit, smiling,
the dead,
who listen with patience to
every utterance of your heart.

Sweet is the presence of the one who no longer hastens.

FROZEN NIGHT

The moon
cruel
was bathing in light
the soft
whiteness of the snow.
People entered the illuminated
cafés.
Voices
intertwined in the road
covered in ice.

And I didn't want to.

The sound of boots in the snow,
music
escaped
from the doors ajar.
Brief laughter
resounded
against the low roofs
of the houses.
The woods were dark,
there beyond the village.
The valley mute in the ice.

And I didn't want to.

The nocturnal
breeze
brushed my face
with its hand of ice.

I did not want to.

My love to die,
like so
on a frozen night.

I did not want to.

MARCH

On a street near my home
there is an old wall that has no windows:
bare, blackened face without eyes,
it does not have bright iridescent glass
to send back the flashing light of the sun;
there is never anyone to rest his gaze upon it.

But when March comes
a tree flowers near the wall
and with pitying fingers,
lightly caresses the hidden
cracks... and through the fresh laughter
of the new season,
that wall too shows a happy face.

So it is with the heart: a word, a lover's nod,
two hands holding each other in silence,
are enough to make a hawthorn
flower among the ruins of a dead garden.

LIBECCIO*

Earth: sweet seaside,
drops of rain from the pines.
Sea: scents of September,
a footprint in the wet sand,
the smashing of the waves on the rocks.
A dead crab.
And us: words in the middle of the *Libeccio*,
the salt taste in the mouth.

the south-west wind, the Scirocco

FRAGMENT 1

Why do I comb my hair
if you're not here?
A fresh apron to tie
around my blue dress
why, if you're not here?
Two roses cut in the garden
I have put in a little vase,
why, if you're not here?

FRAGMENT 2

In your eyes there is the sea,
green at times,
of a blue intensity
when at midday
the *maestrale** blows.

* *maestrale: the north-west wind*

SNAPSHOT

I was passing in the car that day, along an avenue,
watching the people, there, I saw them:
both young, he tall and slim, she blonde.
They had stopped one beside the other.
They looked at one another, and she, lost,
imploring with her sky-blue eyes,
pressed her head against his shoulder,
and fear made her mouth tremble...
He encircled her with his virile arm
and reassured her with a smile.

TWO DAYS IN PARIS

For a short while I saw you:
when the weather causes a rose to decay.
It was the month of April,
uncertain between shine and rain.

Walking down the Champs-Élysées,
from the North the wind blew.
And on high, that sky,
which opens and closes a scene on you,
Prima Donna.

THE YOUNG GIRL OF THE METRO

I saw her on the metro
with the eyes of a gazelle,
a sweet girl,
a slender girl.

I saw her on the metro
she was alone and pensive;
in that noisy darkness
she seemed luminous.

I saw her on the metro:
Is she a dancer?
Or maybe a model?
She is certainly unhappy I know.

I saw her on the metro
with the eyes of a gazelle,
a sweet girl,
a slender girl.

LOOK OF LOVE

We were returning towards home in silence,
the summer's evening – warm, violet –
was caressing the mountains and the pines,
red flashes,
fleeing from the west
were setting the branches alight.
On the sea, the shadow of the night
was slowly falling.
And there, you turned to me:
and I saw your blonde hair
reverberate the red flame
of that sunset:
one look from your brow shot like a dart
and like a blade it pierced my heart.

SUMMER RAIN

Like soldiers in a line
are the cabins
along the empty beach,
guarding the grey sea,
which patiently gathers
the tears of the sky.
A cyclist passes slowly
on the path.
Around the closed windows
a fly buzzes and settles.

ON THE BANK

Wind on the sea...
Your gaze travels as far as the horizon:
in the blue water
I wash my thoughts
and let them climb
towards the sky.
Flying by,
a tender gull.

TO BOB DYLAN

You are right, young man,
yes, you are right
to sing your questions to the people;
to the people who pass hurriedly by
and are afraid to think for themselves.

Your song is like an elegy:
sad, but sweet
to the one who wants to hear it;
it has the soft enchantment of silence
that transports us into eternity.

Your voice,
of a young psalmist,
vibrates with love
for humanity.

HOMER

Along the cool avenues
of the heavenly city,
your face we will know, Homer,
and your fatherland,
and the reason your eyes
were closed,
but throughout the world
you will still be
the unknown, legendary bard,
blind, wandering from city to city,
to sing the deeds of the heroes.

And if we search for your face,
we will always see
among the pink clouds
of your beautiful dawn,
or across the foam of your immense ocean,
now this one, now that one of the heroes,
whom you, great poet, moving yourself to one side,
allow to walk
through all the centuries,
and towards every mortal brother,
who, relishing your poems,
drinks of them.

THE DESERT ROSE

In my hand I hold
and caress
your amber petals of crystal,
O mysterious rose of the desert.
The age-old hand of the wind
worked you,
and the nights dense with stars
and the burning sun.
A solitary wise camel driver
discovered you among the dunes,
and from your secret place
he carried you far away.
Now you are here
and in touching you I seek,
among the sharp
well-proportioned lines
of your graceful form,
the voice of centuries,
and the infinite beauty of creation.

JUNE

The noon-day laughs,
soon it will be evening.
In a longer day
summer will follow spring,
and winter, autumn;
and so on again,
until, in the sky, shines the hot sun.

THE DESERT

Steep cliffs,
flashes of sunlight like fire
and all around the redness of the desert,
sand
sand in your eyes,
sand like blood dust,
and solitude that is as a prayer.

CROSSING THE PO VALLEY

I looked into the evening sky
while autumn discoloured the fields,
and I saw
an angel's wing, light,
one white cloud among the grey,
a shape formed
amidst the formless haze.

My eyes search for nothing else
to dispel the shadows of the night,
no more than the soft beating
of an angel's wing, light,
white smile in the grey evening.

TO BE ELSEWHERE

Heat
bathes the city.
A cry of swallows
in the morning
presses on your temples,
penetrates.

Desire
for far-off paths,
the shadow of chestnut trees
on solitary village fountains
rising from the stone.

Desire
to awaken in a new room,
to run to the window
in bare feet:
walnut tree
in the morning,
a stone wall
at the side of the street.
An old man sits
smoking his pipe,
the outline of the nearest mountains is born.

Desire
to be a child,
and inside
that yearning, always new,
for the day that approaches.

Desire
to plunge my hands into the stream:
freezing water
which cuts at the wrists;
voices of the forest
in the still silence.
On high sings a
chaffinch in the oak tree,
another now responds
in the distance.

THE CHOIR

They sang in harmony:
weary, but their voices carried on.
That evening when the friends before the hearth gathering
still had in their eyes
the cliffs climbed that morning.
And almost like tightrope walking
in a dream on a magic wire dancing,
their new thoughts were wandering,
the banks of the river lightly touching,
from which they had asked to drink the day before;
then refreshed, returning swiftly
along that famous and difficult way,
up there, among the silent peaks,
they had vanished in a light-blue veil.

MAMMA*

What am I thinking of
when I say *mamma**...
I think of a woman
with a tired face
lit by the light of a smile,
and in her look
gushes forth so strong a flame
that the whole of her sweet face
is animated by it;
and on her tender nape
a neat bun of hair,
that one day was black
and was lovely,
she seems wrapped up in all her thoughts,
happy or sad,
or full of sweetness.

* *'mamma' is the term all Italians use for their mother, even formally, so it would be inappropriate to use the equivalent 'mummy','mammy' etc as these are only used informally in English.*

SUMMER TWILIGHT

Motionless are the olive trees
down in the field,
still bright is
the new moon in the sky.
The land stretches out,
the sun is warm.
The crickets sing,
the lane is deserted.
Slowly I go out through the open gate,
I greedily drink of that silence.
I look at the stars
and I surrender to
the slow liquefaction of the hours.
It pays to walk through the eternal spaces,
cradled by the good Mother Earth.

AUTUMN IN TUSCANY

Speak, O walls of the ancient tower
and tell what view you had
from the narrow windows
over the golden valley
so sweet and kind.
Voices of ancient horsemen
and the beating of hooves on the path
where my babies now run.
And I sing of women
who happily contemplated the blue mist
and the golden leaves of nature.
On a still morning like this
one hears only the rooster,
only seldom the shot of a rifle.
And slowly the sun floods the countryside
on this autumn morn, as sweet as it was then.
And the centuries are as nothing.

THE CALL

A long time
I've been far from you,
my land.
Subdued,
among the sharp rocks,
the wind calls.
It passes over your flocks,
your streams,
and calls.
To me a hint is enough
to understand.
Like the stones,
and the tough olives,
the sons of that island
are sparing of words;
but deep,
full of heart and of secret thoughts.
A long time,
I know;
but soon I will return to you.

THE CHOPPED TREE

They have cut off the new growth:
beside its green purity, harsh is the
flashing blade.
Unknowing steps in the road trample
young leaves
that no longer know the tree.

Dreams, born in the morning,
in the evening are dead.

VOICE OF A LITTLE GIRL

The feather-light voice
of a little girl:
sorrowfully you play
the most secret
strings
of my drowsy harp.
You pluck them a little
and then suddenly leave them:
murmur of eternity
inside a cave.

VANITY

You wouldn't know how to create
a trembling blade of grass,
a child's golden curl,
the feather of a white dove.
Why do you dream so much of glory?

You wouldn't know how to create
the aromatic fragrance of myrtle,
a breath of wind that lightly touches
the fresh greenery of the garden.
Why so much conceit?

Not even a drop of sea water
would you know how to create from nothing.
And you sing of victory?

HOPES

The sound of tender accents
rises up
in your thoughts,
young voices
make ripples in the pool
where, at the bottom overturned,
lies the cup of your tears.
And through the intricacy
of the leafy boughs
pass
in the fresh wind of the morning,
hopes
that you recognise
as yours.
Under the tough bark
made by the greed of time,
stirs the sap
of the re-born plant.

WHO AM I?

My mother, who is she?
She kisses me, and doesn't know.
I look and I don't see her.
Whatever is budding inside my son?
I hold him, I smile,
but he is far from me.

And you, who are you, really?
When do you exist?
When are you real?
Do you dream? Do you cry?
Do you hope?
The more you shake
the bars of your bitter cell, shivering,
the more you want to stay there.
The more you delve into your deepest
self, the darker the mystery becomes.

If you think, there is only one way.

KNOW YOURSELF

Today I would like to know myself:
in a fresh drop of dew,
to reflect back intact my new-born soul.
I would like to see it simple,
like a seed,
strong and compact like ancient stone,
lashed by the intemperate weather of centuries,
steady, un-moved, and un-disturbed
by the turmoil which we call life.

STARS

For so much time
I have not seen the stars.
I have forgotten how
to be as nothing.
God was hiding His face
in the mists of time.

THE TEARS OF THE WORLD

Your smile
searches in my eyes
and does not discover there
my muted cry.
So it is that along the stream,
from stone to stone,
flow in silence
the tears of the world.

A PRAYER FOR YOU

Oceans
separate
your pain from my hands,
brother who suffers,
sister who cries.
But when I pray,
I caress your face,
I soften your tears.
And perhaps you feel a sudden warmth:
it is I
that is praying for you.

SIMPLICITY

I dream of the flame in a great fireplace
with a little worn-out bench beside
on which is sitting a rather tired lady
with a stocking already begun in her lap;
and a pot hung on the chain
where there is something boiling for dinner.
Few things, but in all nothing is missing.
If you think, you can count on one hand
those things that are needed for living.

POOR PEOPLE

Dear poor people,
there inside rooms decorated with nothing,
with your mouths adorned with silence,
the flame of a smile to warm you,
burning in the fire of a long suffering,
the *Ave Maria* to console you at dinner,
scrutinising each other's faces,
and finding again courage and hope.

THE SHEPHERD

It was almost dark,
and the shepherd returned home
in slow steps,
together with his tired flock.
And in his gaze,
lost in the distance
are waving fields,
and across the blue sky
white clouds are gently floating.

The long, slow, silent walk
so many of his passions has consumed,
nothing remains but wisdom and love,
and to fill a heart that is more than enough.

SARDINIA

If my foot
one day sinks
in the burning sand,
if I pull my dripping hands
from the blue sea,
while my gaze traces the coastline,
then I will want to say
that I have come to you,
my true land,
Sardinia, never seen,
ever loved.
Then,
like the exile, prostrate,
I will kiss the arid sunburnt soil,
and then, trembling,
I will press my ear
to the opened lips of the rocks,
listening to the voices of my forefathers.

THREE POEMS WRITTEN AT THE AGE OF NINE, 1937:

PIGEONS

On the roof of the school
pigeons and lovebirds
were enjoying the heat of the sun
feeding their little ones.
And I from the opened window of my class
watched them: lightly they flew
and huddled under the eaves.
I saw one then
with his little head bowed
and long I watched him
until he flew,
never more to return into my view.

THE DAISY

O daisy
queen of the fields
little head of golden hair
and white crown, on
the flowering sod
you spend your sweet life.
Teach me your song
I want to sing it every hour
and keep it in my heart forever stored.

THE ROBIN

Little bird of the woods,
you chirp every morning
and stir the fair baby
cradled in that little house.
Come on! Chirp louder!
Spread your song everywhere!
Then fly on to the roof,
go in search of food,
and keep the hunger from your brood!

THREE OF THE 'POEMS FOR MY CHILDREN'
'THROUGH THE EYES OF MY BABIES'

THE LITTLE TIBETAN GOATS

Our uncle has made us a gift
of two lovely kid-goats.
See how they are so sweet,
white and tiny in their little black coats.
Of all the animals on this farm
these we all prefer,
and if they were to run afar
there'd be trouble in the air!
They bleat so loud
bringing pain to our hearts,
we simply cannot resist
all that tender love.
You know morning and evening
we give them to eat
bread and pears and fine bran of wheat,
and they accept everything
which really is so pleasing!

THE SNACK

Crunch crunch goes my slice
of toasted bread,
while I eat it absorbed in thought:
I have a little marmalade
stuck to my finger,
I have another bit here on my chin,
but there is even more on the floor.

FIFTH BIRTHDAY

Tomorrow is my birthday.
But what do you mean 'tomorrow'?
It comes before yesterday,
or after breakfast?
Mummy, up, please,
explain it to me!

I know now, listen to me:
after hurrying through my meal,
now I can sleep, and when I wake up
it's birthday time for me.